First Nature Books

The Fly

Gunilla Ingves

Adam & Charles Black · London

The First Nature Books series

1 The Fly
2 The Ladybird
3 The Grasshopper
4 The Snail
5 The Mushroom
6 The Dandelion

Published by A & C Black (Publishers) Limited
35 Bedford Row, London WC1R 4JH
First published by Natur och Kultur, Sweden
under the series title *Har du sett på...*

This edition arranged with the help of Angus Hudson, London
Filmset by Euroset Typesetting Limited, London
Printed and Bound in Great Britain
by Purnell and Sons (Book Production) Ltd., Paulton, Bristol

Ingves, Gunilla
The Fly.—(First Nature Books)
1. Flies—Juvenile literature
I. Title II. Har du sett på: Flugan. *English*
III. Series
595.77 QL533.2

ISBN 0-7136-2285-7

Can you hear a buzzing noise?
There is a fly on this red flower.

Along comes a male fly. He mates with the female fly on the red flower.

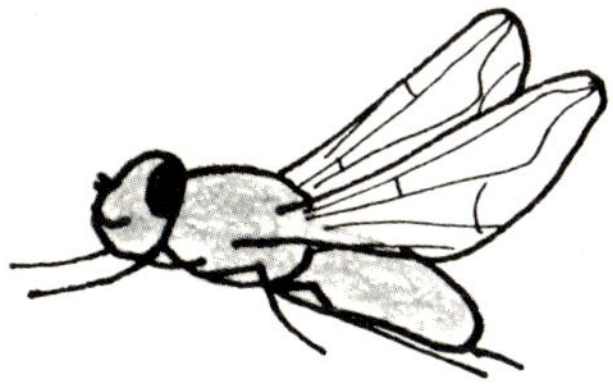

After a week, the female fly lays lots of eggs on a pile of manure. She lays at least a hundred eggs.

The eggs hatch two days later. A maggot crawls out of each egg. The maggots are hungry. They eat everything they can find.

The maggots get fatter and fatter. A hen sees them and, quick as a wink, eats up three of the fattest maggots. Maggots taste sweet to hens.

But some maggots crawl away.

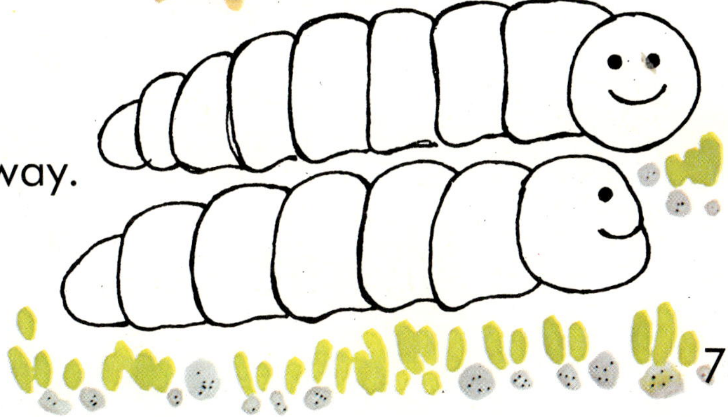

When the maggots can't eat any more, they dig themselves down into the earth and go to sleep.

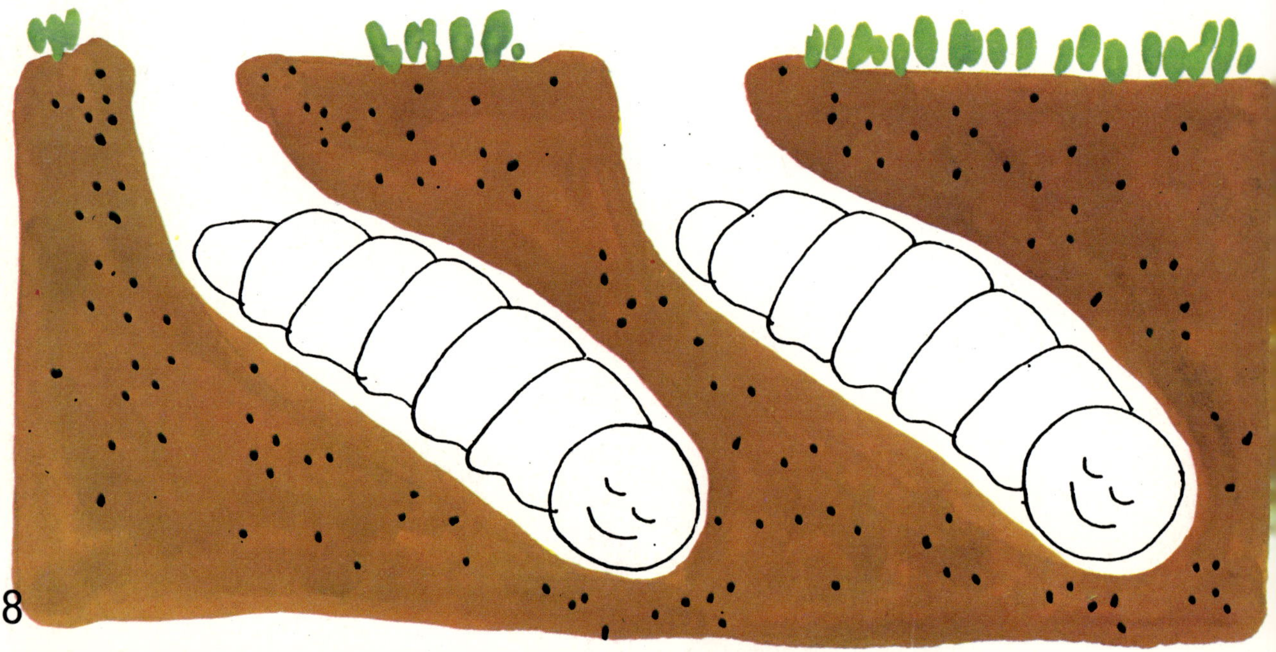

While they are sleeping, their skins become as hard as shells. The shells are called cocoons. The maggots change into flies inside the cocoons.

When the maggots have turned into flies, the cocoons burst. The flies drag themselves out of the soil.

Each fly unfolds its wings and lets the sun dry them. The fly has six jointed legs. Each foot has a sticky pad on it. These pads help the fly to walk on walls and ceilings without falling off.

The fly has big compound eyes. This means that each eye is made from thousands of little eyes. The eyes of a male fly are close together. The eyes of a female fly are further apart.

The fly has two antennae on its head. It uses the antennae to smell. The fly has no mouth or teeth. It sucks up its food in a tube which it can stretch out.

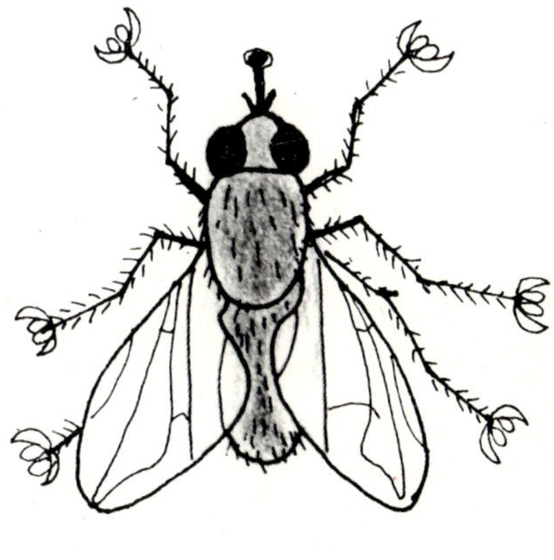

The fly lands on a heap of manure.
There are lots of other flies there, too.

After it has eaten all it can, the fly flies off. It finds an open window and flies in. And there it finds . . .

. . . a huge sticky cake with raspberries and icing.
The fly just has to have a taste!

There is also a cup of coffee with cream. The fly has a taste of that and then has a rest next to the cup. It cleans its feet which are a bit sticky. Then . . .

Wham! A woman tries to kill the fly with a fly-swatter. But the fly escapes

It flies over to the window. The woman is angry with the fly. It has left germs on her cake. She chases the fly but . . .

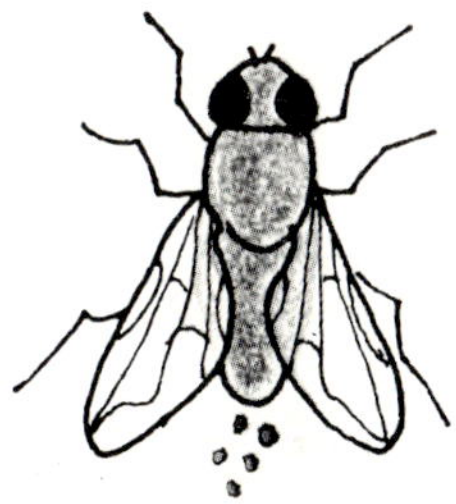

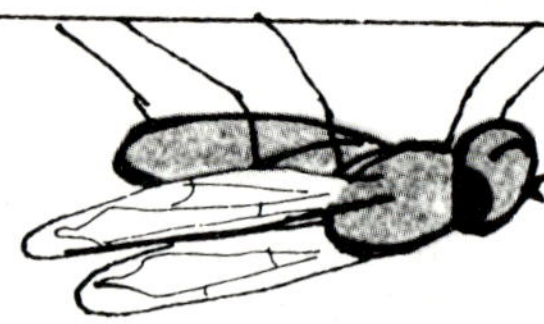

. . . she can't reach up to the ceiling!

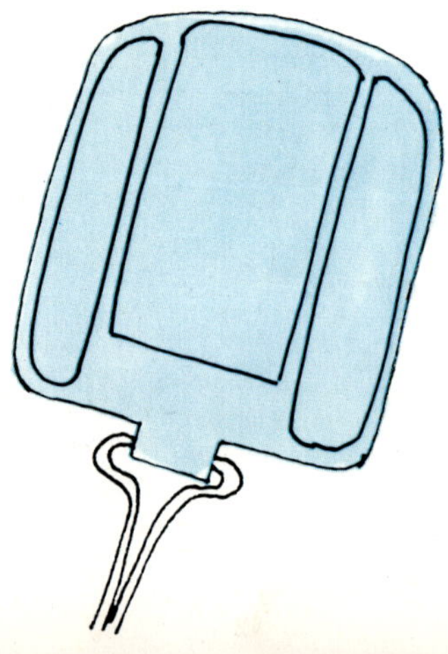

The fly buzzes off through the open window.

A cat is dozing outside in the sunshine. The fly buzzes round the cat. The cat flicks its tail and the fly goes away.

The fly passes a spider's web.
The spider spins a web to catch
flies and other insects. Then it
will eat them.

The fly lands on a warm brick wall. Flies like to sunbathe!

Then it moves on again. It passes a bird which has caught a fly. Flies are good food for young birds.

The fly is feeling hungry again. It lands on another pile of manure and starts to eat.